First published in 2017 by Ginger Fox®
an imprint of Hacche Retail Ltd
Stirling House, College Road, Cheltenham GL53 7HY
United Kingdom

www.gingerfox.co.uk

Follow us!
@GingerFoxUK
@GingerFoxUSA
Tweet us @GingerFox_UK

Compiled by Steve Erdal and Josie Robson for KISS Copy

ISBN: 978-1-911006-25-1

10 9 8 7 6 5 4 3

Printed & Bound in Dongguan, Guangdong, China

MAN
~~Mindfulness~~

It's MINDFULNESS, but for MEN!

MANFULNESS *noun*

1. A MASCULINE MENTAL STATE
ACHIEVED BY FOCUSING ONE'S
AWARENESS ON THE PRESENT
MOMENT, WHETHER WORKING,
ENJOYING FAMILY LIFE OR
GUTTING A STAG LIKE THAT
BLOKE FROM *GAME OF THRONES*.

SLOWLY
GENTLY
DEEPLY*

(*THIS IS A BREATHING TECHNIQUE)

Ahhh

YOU SHOULD NEVER GIVE UP YOUR INNER SELF.

CLINT EASTWOOD

SMILE AT A STRANGER.
YOU MIGHT JUST MAKE THEIR DAY.
OR FREAK THEM OUT.

YOU WIN EITHER WAY.

AS YOU STROLL DOWN THE GARDEN ON YOUR
APPROACH TO THIS HALLOWED PALACE OF
MANFULNESS, CONSIDER THIS:

THERE ARE TREES IN YOUR GARDEN THAT WILL
STILL BE BLOOMING LONG AFTER YOU ARE GONE.
BALANCE ANY NEGATIVE FEELINGS OF INFERIORITY
THIS MAY STIR BY YANKING A FEW LEAVES
OFF THE SMUG GITS.

ENJOY THE PLEASANT SOUND OF BIRDSONG ...
WHILST REMEMBERING THAT IT'S ACTUALLY THE
BIRDS' WAY OF THREATENING TO KILL EACH OTHER.
(BEAUTY AND VIOLENCE IN ALL THINGS.)

WHEN YOU HAVE ARRIVED IN YOUR
TONGUE-AND-GROOVED INNER SANCTUM:

ENSURE THAT YOU HAVE TOTAL SOLITUDE
BY TELLING THE KIDS THAT YOUR LAWNMOWER IS
ALIVE. AND HUNGRY.

MAINTAIN AWARENESS THAT CLUTTER STIFLES
CREATIVITY. NEVER BUY ANY TOOLS. YOU'LL HAVE
MORE ROOM ON YOUR WORKBENCH FOR A FOUR-PACK,
SOME PORK SCRATCHINGS AND A PORTABLE TELLY.

YOUR MANFULNESS WILL SUFFER IF YOU ARE COLD.
FIND SOMETHING, AND BURN IT.
FIRE WILL MAKE EVERYTHING WARM.
YOUR INNER PEACE WILL RETURN.

CHALLENGE YOURSELF.
YOU WILL NEVER KNOW
WHAT YOU'RE CAPABLE
OF UNTIL YOU TRY.

SO WHY NOT ORDER
A SECOND MAIN AND
A COUPLE OF EXTRA
POPPADOMS?

**CHANGE YOUR ROUTINE.
TAKE A DIFFERENT ROUTE TO WORK,
COOK SOMETHING NEW FOR DINNER ...
OR BREAK INTO AREA 51.**

MINDFUL DRINKING

Every pint you drink can be a call to mindfulness and gratitude. If possible, and without a sense of duty, recall how many steps were necessary to create, for example, the lovely pint of real ale in front of you. Freely connect to the farmer who planted and harvested the hops, the brewer who crafted your ale and the lorry driver who kindly delivered the barrel to your local pub.

Really taste the ale. Savour it.
A swift pint can become a feast for your soul
with a little dash of awareness.

Just imagine what the second (or third) pint could do ...

KNOW YOUR AURA COLOURS

**WHAT COLOUR ENERGY ARE YOU EMITTING TODAY?
AND WHAT DOES IT SAY ABOUT YOUR PHYSICAL,
EMOTIONAL AND SPIRITUAL WELLBEING?**

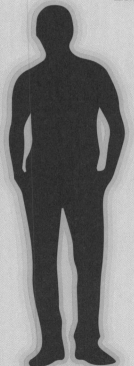

RED: PURE RAGE

ORANGE: YOU ARE TOO ORANGEY FOR CROWS

YELLOW: AURA JAUNDICE (ONE UNIT TOO MANY?)

GREEN: HULK, WILL SMASH

BLUE: LISTENING TO THE SMITHS

PURPLE: CHEWING GUM MISHAP

PINK: SHOWING YOUR FEMININE SIDE

GOLD: ALWAYS BELIEVE IN YOUR SOUL ...

WHITE: LEVEL 2 GANDALF

BE GRATEFUL WITH
EVERYTHING YOU HAVE
AND YOU WILL BE
SUCCESSFUL IN
EVERYTHING YOU DO.

CONNOR MCGREGOR

AROMATHERAPY WORD SEARCH

INHALE DEEPLY AND IMMERSE YOURSELF
IN THE MUSKY, MEATY AROMAS OF MANHOOD ...

BACON	NAPALM
BARBECUE	NUT BROWN ALE
BONFIRE	PETROL
CIGAR	POLLUTION
COFFEE	PUB
CRICKET BALL	SALT
DEEP HEAT	SAWDUST
EXHAUST	SCOTCH
GUNSMOKE	STEAK
MUSK	VINDALOO

```
N S C O T C H S N C T W D C P S
C V A U A O E A N T N O E L M L
R N U T B R O W N A L E E E U L
L A D C O A E D R T L R P U S O
M B A G R A D U R U L I H C K O
R E H V S I B S N O R F E E M S
N N N B P E C T U A T N A B L P
T V T O G O K K R E W O T R A N
L S I L C P L O E A A B K A P B
C D U N A A E L M T G T L B A K
S D L A D S B T U S B I A G N C
O L P P H A A U R T N A C N E B
T O A L L X L C N O I U L C R U
C O F F E E E O K L L O G L O B
F S S S T E A K O T A E N I L U
I C H A U P A K O T S L B C N P
```

**TURN THE
OTHER CHEEK.**

**IT'LL WIND THE
OTHER GUY UP
EVEN MORE.**

I'M NOT GOD
BUT IF I WERE GOD,
THREE QUARTERS OF YOU
WOULD BE GIRLS,
AND THE REST WOULD BE
PIZZA AND BEER.

AXL ROSE

PALACE OF MANFULNESS #2
THE TOILET CUBICLE AT WORK

ENJOY THE SOUND OF RUNNING WATER.
VISUALISE ITS JOURNEY TO THE OCEAN,
AND ALL THE WONDERFUL THINGS
IT WILL PASS ON ITS WAY.

WITH EACH FLUSH OF THE LOO,
PICTURE YOUR WORRIES DISAPPEARING
ROUND THE U-BEND.

IF THE PERSON IN THE NEXT CUBICLE IS STRAINING
AND GRUNTING, DON'T FEEL ANNOYED OR REVOLTED.
CONGRATULATE YOURSELF ON YOUR SUPERIOR
CHOICES WITH REGARD TO FIBRE AT BREAKFAST.

IF YOUR COLLEAGUES HAVE SCRAWLED
ON THE WALLS, USE THE GRAFFITI
IN THE PLAYGROUND OF YOUR IMAGINATION.
PRETEND YOU HAVE DISCOVERED
THE CAVE MARKINGS OF A PRIMITIVE
AND GENITAL-FOCUSED CIVILISATION.

SPEND TIME IN THE PRESENT.
COUNT YOUR BLESSINGS.
BLESSING 1: YOU'RE GETTING PAID RIGHT NOW.

HYGGE IS COSINESS AND CONVIVIALITY CHARACTERISTIC OF DANISH CULTURE. EMBRACE IT BY EATING BACON, SOLVING MURDERS AND WATCHING FILTH ON THE INTERNET.

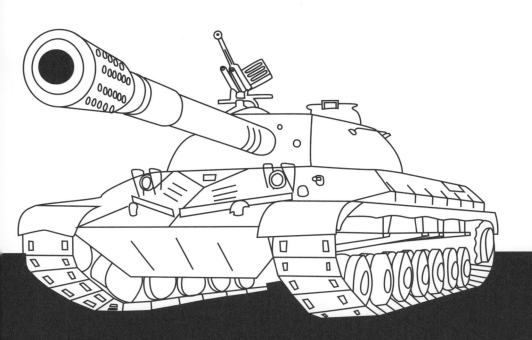

COLOURING AIDS MENTAL CLARITY .... BOOM!

MINDFUL BREAKFAST BUFFET

On your arrival at the breakfast buffet in a hotel, take a moment. Breathe. Remember the broader context for your meal. Specifically, that you can make back the entire hotel bill in sausages.

Don't rush straight to the meat. Take the time to examine the fruit bowl, the granola, the selection of juices. Then, obviously, rush straight to the bacon. We're mindful, we're not insane.

And remember, excess is the antithesis of mindfulness. Take only what you really need, enjoy what you have, treasure the ... hang on a minute IS THAT A WAFFLE IRON??

THE FIRST RULE OF VEGAN CLUB: TELL EVERYONE ABOUT VEGAN CLUB.

SCHWARZENEGGER & STALLONE WORD SEARCH

**FIND YOURSELF WHILST FINDING CHARACTERS
ESSAYED BY NOTED SPIRITUAL TEACHERS ARNOLD
SCHWARZENEGGER AND SYLVESTER STALLONE:**

BENEDICT	MAUSER
COBRA	QUAID
CONAN	RAMBO
DREDD	ROCKY
DUTCH	ROSS
FREEZE	SPARTAN
HATCH	STARHAWK
KIMBLE	TANGO
KOVAK	TASKER
MATRIX	TERMINATOR

```
C T C O U R D I A N N I R S K T
U K W A H R A T S N C E T R I S
A T A A B R O I F O S S R N M I
N T T T S Q O H L U E O D I B A
U A T O R D E T A D M Z Z O L D
R R T L G K U M A T Z M E K E E
O O K R A N B D S N C C R E D S
C O S V A R A B R T I H E I R A
T N O S M P E T K O H M M D G F
A K H Y T B S K R U C B R R Z E
O B M A R C M W S K K K E E Q X
B E N E D I C T R A I Q Y D T K
B M H C T U D S I S T C T D A O
N M A T R I X E C O B R A M T K
I D I A U Q N A N O C O D T A S
H A Y D C I B R K M E Q H C B I
```

KNOW YOUR YOGA

HEAVY FOOT ON A WINDY DAY

THE SPEED-SKATING MISHAP

THE CROTCH BALANCE

THE PIRATE SURRENDERING

29

IF YOU SPEND TOO MUCH TIME THINKING ABOUT A THING, YOU'LL NEVER GET IT DONE.

BRUCE LEE

RECLAIM
YOUR INNER
NARRATIVE.

(OR IF YOU CAN'T DO THAT,
SAY IT IN MORGAN FREEMAN'S VOICE.)

SOME MINDFULNESS CLASSES USE WHITE NOISE
TO HELP PUPILS FIND PEACE AMIDST CHAOS.
YOU CAN ACHIEVE THE SAME EFFECT
WITH STEVE WRIGHT'S AFTERNOON SHOW.

PAY ATTENTION TO THE AROMAS IN YOUR CAR.
REALLY EXPLORE THE DIZZYING AND NUANCED
COCKTAIL OF BURNING OIL, ROTTING BANANA
SKIN AND TODDLER VOMIT.

AS AN EXPERIMENT,
TRY DRIVING JUST BELOW THE SPEED LIMIT.
RELISH THE JOYFUL HARMONY OF HORNS
RINGING OUT BEHIND YOU.

IF SOMEONE CUTS YOU UP,
ACCEPT THAT THIS IS MERELY THE UNIVERSE
TESTING YOUR POWERS OF MINDFULNESS.
RESIST THE TEMPTATION TO GET
OUT OF YOUR CAR AT THE NEXT LIGHTS
AND SLAP THEM WITH YOUR CHAMOIS LEATHER.
UNLESS THEY HAVE A PERSONALISED NUMBER
PLATE, IN WHICH CASE THE UNIVERSE
WON'T BLAME YOU.

TAKE RISKS

IF YOU WIN, YOU WILL BE HAPPY.

IF YOU LOSE, YOU WILL BE WISE.

IF YOU DRAW, YOU WILL BE WEST BROM.

(PROBABLY)

JOIN THE DOTS ... CONNECT WITH THE NOW.

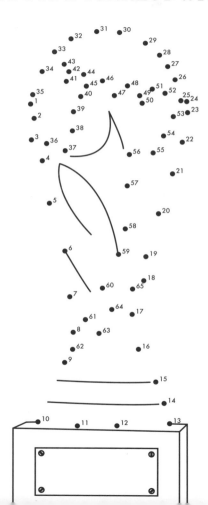

DON'T JUDGE YOUR THOUGHTS.

ACKNOWLEDGE YOUR URGE
TO DISMEMBER YOUR BOSS WITH A KATANA
AND THROW HIS ENTRAILS INTO THE SEA.

THEN MOVE ON.

WE'VE ALL GOT OUR
SELF-DESTRUCTIVE BAD HABITS,
THE TRICK IS TO FIND FOUR OR FIVE
YOU PERSONALLY LIKE THE BEST AND
JUST DO THOSE ALL THE TIME.

DAVID LEE ROTH

MONSTER TRUCK WORD SEARCH

LET THESE CHARIOTS OF MANFULNESS TRANSPORT YOU TO YOUR SPECIAL PLACE:

ANNIHILATOR
ARACHNOPHOBIA
AVENGER
BACKDRAFT
BALLISTIC
BARBARIAN
BIG CRUNCH
BRUTUS
CRUSHSTATION
FLUFFY

FULLBOAR
KNUCKLEHEAD
MCGRUFF
PODZILLA
REPTOID
SCORPION
SHREDDER
TAZ
VOODOO
XTERMIGATOR

```
A L O C P O D P L N R X V E O F
T N P V O O D O O B T C A P F B
T Y O O D R E G N E V A M H P U
B E T A Z T F A R D K C A B U I
B S A F I O C M Y D R K C R C V
R R B O L B I G C R U N C H S U
O C U I L G O D F F L U F F Y R
N O I T A T S H S U R C R R I R
K O N T U R R R P H L K X I O F
B R O F S S E G R O R L N P S K
I R I R T I A P O D N E B S O B
P C P H H A L L T G K H D O F L
R P R R P E C L R O A E C D A Z
I A O S B A R B A R I A N A E R
K M C G R U F F N B C D R L R R
B L S H E R O T A L I H I N N A
```

ALTERNATIVE ALTERNATIVE THERAPIES

Always be on the look-out for new therapeutic treatments
that might just help you achieve transcendental manfulness.
Why not give one of these (totally genuine) therapies a try?

BEE STING THERAPY
Apparently, bee venom has anti-inflammatory properties.
So, basically, you go into a clinic and pay some guy to sting
you with bees. Sting away the pain. Buzz-arre.

COSMIC ORDERING
The one Noel Edmunds was into,
before he moved on to the psychic helpline for dogs.

FIRE FACIAL
Huǒ Liáo fire treatments are gaining popularity in China. Simply soak a towel in alcohol, drape it over your face and set it on fire. Enlightening.

CUDDLE THERAPY
Exactly as it sounds. But the therapist probably doesn't look like you're imagining.

BEER SPA
Bathing in beer. Beer spas are common in the Czech Republic, Germany and Austria. Sounds good in theory, but it doesn't get you drunk and probably makes the beer taste of verrucas.

FASTING THERAPY
Nope.

THE JAPANESE SAY YOU HAVE THREE FACES.
THE FIRST FACE, YOU SHOW TO THE WORLD,
THE SECOND YOU SHOW TO YOUR FAMILY,
AND THE THIRD YOU SHOW ONLY TO YOURSELF.

YOU CAN CALL THESE FACES BLUE STEEL,
LE TIGRE AND MAGNUM.

MINDFUL GOLFING

The tranquillity of a golf course is the perfect place to work on your mindfulness. Admire the majestic arc of the ball as it veers into the woods. Enjoy the playful chirrup of the birds on the green, completely undisturbed by your shanked approach shot.

Lose yourself in the ever-expanding ripples as your ball sinks into the water hazard.

For devotees of eastern religion, you may also get a glimpse of the Buddha while you golf. At the very least, you'll see some rotund, contented balding men.

BE.
HERE.
NOW.

(IT'S MORE THAN AN OASIS ALBUM.)

IF YOU CAN FIND A PATH WITH NO OBSTACLES, IT PROBABLY DOESN'T LEAD ANYWHERE.

BEAR GRYLLS

EVEN IN THE QUIETEST CARRIAGE, THERE ARE SOUNDS FOR YOU TO EXPLORE. CONCENTRATE ON THE RHYTHMIC RATTLE AND HUM OF THE ROLLING STOCK, THE WHOOSH AS YOU PASS THROUGH A TUNNEL, THE HEN-PARTY IN THE NEXT CARRIAGE ...

TRAIN SEATS ARE ESPECIALLY DESIGNED TO MAKE YOU MORE MINDFUL OF YOUR BODY. PARTICULARLY YOUR KNEES.

AS THE TROLLEY WHEELS BY, APPRECIATE THE COLOURS OF THE PRODUCE, IMAGINE THE FLAVOURS AND TEXTURES IN YOUR MOUTH, AND DECIDE WHICH KIDNEY YOU'D SELL IN ORDER TO ACTUALLY BUY SOMETHING.

THE STILLNESS OF FALLEN LEAVES ENRICHES THE SOUL. AND NOWHERE DO FALLEN LEAVES CAUSE MORE STILLNESS THAN ON BRITISH TRAINS.

I HAVE MADE A LOT OF MISTAKES.
BUT I'VE WORKED HARD.
I HAVE NO FEAR OF DEATH.
MORE IMPORTANT, I DON'T FEAR LIFE.

STEVEN SEAGAL

COLOUR YOURSELF CALM ...
RELEASE YOUR INNER ROAR!

**THE BIGGEST WALL YOU'VE GOT TO CLIMB
IS THE ONE YOU BUILD IN YOUR MIND.**

**UNLESS YOU'RE
SPIDER-MAN.**

MINDFUL WRESTLING

Always wrestle in the present.

Find a moment mid-elbow drop
to appreciate the pull of gravity on your body.

Pause mid-headlock to tune in to your senses.

Pay attention to your breathing.
Sense the flow of the breath, the rise and fall of your belly.
Then clothesline The Rock so hard his eyebrows fly off.

YOU WILL

REST IN PEACE.

THE UNDERTAKER

YOUR CHAKRAS SHOULD ALWAYS BALANCE.

IF THEY DON'T YOU'LL WALK FUNNY.

THERE IS MINDFULNESS IN LAUGHTER.
THERE IS MINDFULNESS IN TEARS.

SO I GUESS YOU'RE WATCHING *TOY STORY 2*, AGAIN.

MINDFUL MEALS

Never underestimate the power of eating mindfully.

What does the food look like? Smell like? Taste like?
What does it feel like in your mouth?

If the answer to all of those questions is 'pork'
then you're winning.

IF YOU CAN CHANGE YOUR MIND,
YOU CAN CHANGE YOUR LIFE.
(WHICH MAKES YOUR GIRLFRIEND
A FREAKING SUPERHERO.)

PALACE OF MANFULNESS #5
THE FOOTBALL STADIUM

WHEN BITING INTO THE HALF-TIME PIE,
GIVE A MOMENT OF THANKS TO THE COWS
THAT GAVE THEIR LIPS AND GONADS
TO PROVIDE YOU WITH ESSENTIAL SUSTENANCE.

REMEMBER, BEING FOULED IS A STATE OF MIND.
THAT'S WHY THEIR NUMBER 7 CAN BE FOULED
WITHOUT ANY CONTACT WHATSOEVER.

INCOHERENT RAGE DOES NOT
BELONG IN THE CONSCIOUS MIND.
IT BELONGS ON ARSENAL FAN TV.

MUSIC CAN
CHANGE YOUR MOOD
AND MAKE
TASKS EASIER.
FOR INSTANCE,
LISTEN TO
ED SHEERAN
WHEN YOU HAVE TO
PICK UP A DOG POO.
AND THE DOG POO'S
ON FIRE.

MINDFUL FOOTBALL CHANTS

Chants are a wonderful way of generating
that wholesome feeling of togetherness with your fellow
fans, but some of the content can corrupt your path
to manfulness.

So here are some alternatives:

"You're not singing,
You're not singing,
YOU'RE not singing any more!
(It's not a criticism, we just want to check you're OK.)"

"Who ate all the pies?
Who ate all the pies?
We've got quinoa, we've got quinoa,
So don't worry about it."

"Sacked in the morning!
You're getting sacked in the mooooorning!
But when one door closes another opens."

"The referee is at ease with his own sexuality and able to
explore the pleasures of his own body."

GRASS GROWS,
BIRDS FLY,
WAVES POUND THE SAND.
I BEAT PEOPLE UP.

MUHAMMAD ALI

MINDFULLNESS IS

ALL ABOUT NOTICING THE

THE LITTLE DETAILS.

HI.

AXEMAN WORD SEARCH

**THERE IS NO MORE MINDFUL MUSIC
THAN THE OPENING RIFF OF *SWEET CHILD OF MINE*.**

BERRY
COBAIN
EDGE
FRANCIS
FRUSCIANTE
GREENWOOD
HAMMETT
HENDRIX
IOMMI
KNOPFLER

MARR
MAY
PAGE
RICHARDS
SLASH
TOWNSHEND
VAN HALEN
WATERS
YOUNG
ZAPPA

```
O T S A I A S C Z A W A T E R S
L E W I O T E S A P E S R R Y R
I O V E C D A E Z A L E C N E I
T S A M G N I Y R R E B E A H W
D L N E P E A G H E N D R I X N
O A H Y H A T R E L F P O N K M
O S A E O D G N F S S A D U M P
W H L D C U M E A E N Y O T W G
N G E C N R N A Y I I M T R I D
E I N S E S M G Y H C E U T O D
E D G N I A B O C K M S H I M M
R I C H A R D S O M N R U U M A
G N T A B E A N A S A H N R I R
E E B N A E S H S E H N N H F R
E R C T O W N S H E N D E O P M
T A L R N P E Z A P P A S P H T
```

FOR EVERY DARK NIGHT,
THERE'S A BRIGHTER DAY.

TUPAC SHAKUR

TRUST BEFORE YOU LOVE.

KNOW BEFORE YOU JUDGE.

FORGIVE BEFORE YOU FORGET.

APPRECIATE BEFORE YOU REGRET.

LOOK BEFORE YOU ZIP.

YOUR MIND IS A GARDEN. YOUR THOUGHTS ARE THE SEEDS.
YOU CAN GROW FLOWERS OR YOU CAN GROW WEEDS.

(AND DON'T FORGET, YOU CAN KILL IT IF IT BLEEDS.)

PAY ATTENTION TO YOUR PARTNER'S BODY LANGUAGE
WHEN YOU'RE TALKING TO HER.
FOR EXAMPLE, IF SHE PUNCHES YOU IN THE STOMACH,
YOU SHOULD PROBABLY POSTPONE THAT ROUND OF GOLF TODAY.

COMPETITIVENESS

WILL SUCK YOU DRY.

BE THE LEAST COMPETITIVE PERSON

IN THE WHOLE WIDE WORLD.

MEN ARE LIKE STEEL.
WHEN THEY LOSE
THEIR TEMPER,
THEY LOSE THEIR WORTH.

CHUCK NORRIS

PALACE OF MANFULNESS #6
THE AIR DUCTS IN NAKATOMI TOWER

AIR DUCTS ARE A FANTASTIC PLACE TO
RECALIBRATE AFTER A BUSY CHRISTMAS EVE
DODGING MACHINE-GUN-TOTING EUROPEANS.

CROSS-STITCH IS AN EXCELLENT ACTIVITY FOR
ENCOURAGING MINDFULNESS. REMEMBER THIS
WHEN SEWING YOUR SHOULDER BACK ON.

THE ECHOEY AIR DUCTS WILL PRESENT
THE PERFECT OPPORTUNITY FOR YOU TO
WORK ON YOUR YOGIC CHANTS.

USE THE PEACE AND QUIET TO COME UP WITH A REALLY EXCELLENT LINE FOR WHEN YOU THROW THE RINGLEADER OFF THE TOP OF THE TOWER. "YIP-KIY-YAY SOMETHING" MAYBE. BUT LESS SILLY.

NINJA DOT-TO-DOT

CLEAR YOUR MIND.

CLEAR YOUR DIARY.

MOST IMPORTANTLY,

CLEAR YOUR WEB HISTORY.

IN THE YEAR 3000
PEOPLE WILL TALK TO EACH
OTHER WITH SOUND WAVES.
DON'T THINK I'M CRAZY, THE
WHALES DO IT, DOLPHINS TOO.

JEAN-CLAUDE VAN DAMME

MINDFUL WEREWOLF TRANSFORMATION

So you've been bitten by a wolf, and now you're experiencing all-over body hair and bloodlust? It doesn't mean that you can't still practise mindfulness.

Watch the beautiful, full white moon and imagine the moonlight's journey, from the sun to the moon, down to Earth and onto your hunched and bristling shoulders.

Ensure that you control your emotions at all times, or the worst may happen and you could end up as the love interest in a teen romantic horror movie.

MANFULNESS GLOSSARY

AROMATHERAPY:
A MASSAGE FROM FRANCESCO TOTTI

ASTRAL PROJECTION:
DOING A POWERPOINT PRESENTATION IN THE
BACK SEAT OF AN OLD VAUXHALL

CHAKRA:
YODELLING COLUMBIAN MENTALIST

HAIKU:
A JAPANESE LIMERICK

HYGGE:
OLD DANISH FOR 'MONEYSPINNER'

MANFULNESS GLOSSARY

QI:
THAT SHOW THAT USED TO BE HOSTED BY STEPHEN FRY

REIKI:
A BIT LIKE A RAKE

SPIRIT ANIMAL:
A MOLE IN A BOTTLE OF VODKA

TAO:
BRUMMIE TOE

TRANSCENDENTAL:
TRANSFORMER TEETH

MINE'S A PINT ... AND A PACKET OF FELT-TIPS!

HOMEOPATHY TEACHES US
THAT THE SMALLEST PARTICLES
CAN HAVE THE MOST POWER.
(AT LEAST THAT'S WHAT
YOUR GIRLFRIEND SAID.)

ALWAYS LIVE IN THE MOMENT.
NEVER LIVE IN NORWICH.